THE CONCISE *Graphology* NOTEBOOK

Patricia Marne is Founder Member and Chairwoman of the Graphology Society and she has written several other books which you may enjoy.

Graphology 'Teach Yourself Books', Hodder & Stoughton, 1980 (Fourth Impression 1986)

Crime and Sex in Handwriting, Constable, 1981

The Secret's in Their Signature, Foulsham, 1986
Reveal the Secrets in Doodles, Foulsham, 1987

THE CONCISE *Graphology* NOTEBOOK

PATRICIA MARNE

W. Foulsham & Co. Ltd.
London • New York • Toronto •
Cape Town • Sydney

W. Foulsham & Company Limited
Yeovil Road, Slough, Berkshire, SLI 4JH

ISBN 0-572-01449-X

Printed in Great Britain at
Edmundsbury Press, Bury St Edmunds

CONTENTS

Your handwriting is all-revealing. To the trained eye it lays open your secret mind. Every whirl or line you pen exposes your true character and personality to the graphologist.

By knowing ourselves through our handwriting we can avoid doing some things that aren't right for us. By knowing our potential, our weaknesses and our strengths, we are less likely to take on too much, or even too little.

Handwriting analysis can help you in your search for whatever it is you want out of life. So take up your pen and see if your handwriting shows you to be optimistic or pessimistic, introverted or extroverted.

This book will enable you to use graphology as a guide to knowing yourself and others just that much better. To know one's limitations in life is a great asset, and to know the heights one can attain is also a great help.

You can make a determined effort to get rid of negative thoughts by thinking positively. This is going to show in your handwriting which will be more confident — and so will you.

FORM LEVEL

Form level is the primary impression one forms of the writing before studying individual letters and strokes. It shows the writer's whole personality, revealing intelligence and maturity or immaturity.

Assessing form level is not easy and takes considerable experience. When the overall look of the handwriting has been appraised, the graphologist can venture on and evaluate each single trait revealed in the script sample.

The complexities of human nature are many and varied, and no more clearly is this illustrated than in handwriting. Therefore the graphologist will need a combination of experience and intuition as he or she will be frequently confronted by contradictory traits. This is also why it is essential that a knowledge of psychology is incorporated into the study of graphology. Many eminent psychologists and psychiatrists, including Carl Jung and Freud, have shown an interest in and studied graphology with positive findings. They have found that expressive movements in handwriting are as revealing as a person's physical movements and gestures, because both are performed without being conscious that such actions can be interpreted as indications of character. No matter how you disguise your handwriting, your individual traits will always be detected by the trained eye of the graphologist.

When you write a note in a hurry or take your time writing a special letter, you will think that the two pieces of writing are different, that the slowly written letter will be easier to read and neater to look at — but both will have the same characteristics.

Why handwriting should reveal these details of someone's character and personality we don't really know, except that brain writing is another name for handwriting because like any other unconscious movement of the human body, directions sent from the brain dictate the action of the hand. These expressive movements are an accurate guide to interpreting the writer's character.

THE THREE ZONES

Graphologists divide handwriting into three zones. They are:

the upper zone
the middle zone
the lower zone

It is the way you deal with these three zones that reveals your mental, social and emotional characteristics, and even your sexual actions and preferences.

The three zones will reveal whether we are dealing with a person basically idealistic and a perfectionist or one who is normal and realistic.

Is he living in a highly analytical world or is he firmly rooted in a down-to-earth world of material values? We have a similar notion when we unconsciously classify people as spiritual (intellectual) or material according to faces, i.e. dominating forehead or dominating lower part.

Personal maturity is reflected in the proportions of the upper and lower zones to the middle zone. Maturity prevents exaggerated deviations — self-limitation is a prerequisite for top performance.

Maturity requires a balance between high and low, reason and intellect. This balance expresses the genuine organiser. Emphasis of one zone must mean a loss in others, resulting in one-sidedness. The neglected area requires equal consideration.

The upper zone

The upper zone reflects and symbolises meditation, abstraction and speculation, unfettered by material considerations. It shows the striving and idealistic qualities: imagination, vision, seeking after perfection. It is linked with the super-ego (conscience and self-criticism).

Middle zone

The middle zone symbolises the balance between cultural and instinctual desires. It represents the rational social conscience and the sentiments. It measures the adaptability to everyday reality and the social attitudes of the writer.

Lower zone

This is the sphere of primitive instincts, or irrationality. The material demands of self-preservation are found here as well as submerged mental tendencies (emotion), sexual tendencies and habits.

LEGIBILITY

The legibility of handwriting is, of course, immediately obvious. Those whose work requires meticulous attention to detail are more likely to present a clear and uniform script than those who are in more creative work.

A **legible** script reveals sincerity and purposefulness, careful attention to detail, clear communication and comprehension. On the negative side, it can also reveal a lack of strong impulses, and poor vision and foresight, the writer living in a rather narrow world and rarely capable of originality.

An **illegible** script shows carelessness and mistrust, sometimes insincerity, and a general lack of cooperation. On the more positive side, it can show confidentiality and discretion, flexibility and intuition, combined with a desire for full freedom of action.

THE FOUR BASIC FORMATIONS

There are four basic formations in handwriting analysis. They are angular, arcade, garland and thread.

Angular script is rigid, controlled and disciplined, showing that the writer finds it hard to adapt and is inclined to be uncompromising. These strokes also show a firm, determined and sometimes quarrelsome disposition. Unyielding and hard, the writer allows his head to rule his heart.

Garland writing is easy to perform and shows adaptability and a basically non-aggressive personality. The writer is receptive and responsive to emotion and will dislike any form of friction in his life. Often taking the line of least resistance, he can lack push and drive, particularly in the career area.

Arcade writing indicates a person who is hard to know well and who hides behind a very formal attitude. Often kind but shy, such a writer is socially conventional and is quite likely to have a creative streak. The higher the arcade is made, the more likely the writer is to be artistic. Many people in the arts, and especially music, have such formations in their small **n**'s and **m**'s.

Thread writing is a sign of the manipulator who is skilled in evading responsibilities. It is often found in the handwriting of opportunists. Because it is an indication of a clever and versatile mind, such writers can be intuitive and are able to influence other people.

Garland writing explained

Garland handwriting is basically a non-aggressive script, showing adaptability and a natural spontaneity. It is usually a feminine script and although the writer may be confident and socially responsive there is a slight tendency under conflict to lack firm discipline and to be easily led by a stronger personality.

Garland writers seek to avoid conflict and have more easygoing natures than any of the other connecting strokes. Receptive, sympathetic and approachable, there can be an indecisive quality about them. They are sometimes fickle and irresolute, which makes them seem more dependent than they are.

Because garland writing is an almost effortless motion, in some graphology books it is said to reveal laziness and a certain fickleness. However, this is not always so, especially if there are occasional angles in the handwriting.

When the garlands are made with some pressure they denote warmth and increased vitality; when they are light and broad they show that the writer is generous.

Flat, weak garlands frequently show a good natured personality with a susceptibility to outside influences. The writer can be too compassionate.

Arcade handwriting explained

There is a lack of ease in the arcade script which stresses form and deportment, both socially and aesthetically, but rarely discloses the writer's inner life.

Arcade writing reveals an inner independence and a profound structural sense, with caution and even secretiveness at times.

Alert and watchful, arcade writers are frequently mistrustful and test their friendships before acceptance. A certain formalism may check spontaneity in relationships, and if the arcades are narrow they can reveal a degree of inhibition.

High arcades often denote an artistic or creative streak, even musical talent.

Very shallow arcades belong to the schemer who would sham for his own ends, and who would feign amiability in order to deceive.

Emotionally the arcade writer may be isolated or reserved and yet have depth of feeling concealed beneath a calm and impenetrable attitude.

Angular writing explained

Because angular handwriting is a disciplined movement, it can express a refusal to adapt or difficulty in compromising, believing that firmness is all.

It shows a capacity for persistence and a rather rigid, controlled personality, strong minded but often defensive. The writer is usually unyielding and determined, with a restrictive attitude and fixed ideas and opinions.

When the writing is angular and extremely regular it can reveal sternness and a sense of obligation that is sometimes without tolerance or humour.

More reliable than gracious, the angular writer can be aggressive and suspicious, occasionally seeking to impose his will on others.

When the writing is angular and irregular, it can show misguided resolution and extreme stubbornness, possibly from some inner conflict.

Thread writing explained

Thread writing is very difficult to analyse because of its very formation. It is inclined to dissolve into a line. Most thread writers are quite quick thinking individuals with considerable talent for manipulating and some skill in understanding the motives of others.

Thread writing generally lacks clarity, and very often this means the writer tends to be adaptable but at the cost of having no clear course of action. This indefinite linkage of letters can often reveal a multiplicity of talents, even creativity.

Such writers receive their impressions from everywhere and see everything. Their intelligence is combined with intuition and perception, so much so that they frequently disregard established forms of behaviour. They are ready for any situation, and are clever at extricating themselves from difficulties, employing an evasive strategy in order to gain their own ends.

Thread writers are frequently involved in the arts or creative areas where their mental agility and versatility can take them to the top of their career.

Some thread writers, who are inclined to have poor pressure, are liable to avoid strong or complex situations by side-stepping issues.

Very heavy thread denotes the writer who dislikes routine and who refuses to be chained down to traditional rules and regulations. He feels he must be free to follow his ideas and instincts.

When the thread writing slopes upwards and to the right, it reveals optimism and a well developed social sense, enabling the writer to mix and communicate with ease.

Most thread writing is found in the reasonably educated. It is rare for an uneducated person to have thread writing as it requires speed of thought and fluency of mind. Confidence tricksters have been found to have this type of script as they are opportunists and know exactly when and where to turn their accomplished dishonesty to account. They cannot be pinned down easily and are eloquent, plausible and extremely rapid thinking.

When the thread writing dissolves into almost a line, this may show a certain lawlessness in the character. The owner of this hand is commonly unprincipled or neurotic. Open to receive impressions from people, places and the environment, the thread writer tends to be vacillating.

In the career area, the thread writer makes an excellent journalist, salesman, negotiator or public relations man or woman. His or her strength is in their ability to adapt under any circumstances and to overcome conventional considerations.

Their weaknesses are a tendency to manipulate and to juggle with the truth and they may also lack stamina for long periods of effort, particularly indicated if the pressure is weak.

When thread writing slopes downwards it can be a sign of a writer whose interpretation of law and order means *his* law and order, but it can also indicate mild depression.

This very fast writing shows a thread writer with considerable mental skill and an agile mind. The drooping lines indicate pessimism and the arc-like **i** dot is a sign of excellent powers of observation.

The light pressure shows a lack of energy and vitality. A highly sensitive and critical personality but one who should never be underestimated.

The thread strokes in this specimen of script are at the end of the words, indicating diplomacy and tact. The writer is impatient and irritable under pressure, inclined to rush and doesn't like too many details to pin her down.

The straight downstrokes are indicative of good judgement and an ability to get down to essentials quickly and with the minimum of fuss.

This pasty writing with its heavy pressure shows the writer is fond of eating and drinking, and the pleasures of the senses. The left slant reveals opposition against prevailing ideas and the flat thread strokes show considerable manipulating ability, and a talent for getting her own way.

The thick **t** bar crossing signifies a rather dominant personality. She can be obstinate and wayward under pressure.

This hearty right-slanted handwriting is a little more firmly written, as there are signs of angularity in the strokes, showing a dominant and even mildly aggressive personality. Although the script is flexible and released it is also full of slanting strokes, showing that the writer is a little more cautious than he appears to be at first glance.

MARGINS

Margins have a special significance in graphology. Very few people are aware of deliberately taking care in their presentation. Only the artistic person or the aesthete will take note of the impression their margins are going to make on the reader.

The margins act as a frame round the handwriting. Look at the sample of writing and the paper as a picture and see if it is evenly spaced, well placed and pleasing to the eye. The way you form your margins reveals a lot about your social attitudes and how you react to the world around you.

Wide margin at top of page

If this is wide and generous, you may be rather informal in your manner and prefer your friends and partner to take the initiative as you don't like to make the first move. Your lack of confidence could cause you to doubt your own abilities and lose out on opportunities, especially in the emotional stakes.

Wide margin at bottom of page

If your lower margin is very wide, this may show that you have a fear of your emotions. You could have been hurt or rejected in the past and are frightened of becoming too involved. Standing on the sidelines means that you are often lonely and need to mix and socialise more. You are also intuitive, perceptive and a good listener.

Wide margin at right of page

Sensitive, highly strung and apprehensive about the future, you aren't an easy person to get close to. You are the one-partner type and that's for keeps. A rather serious nature means that you don't like crowds and prefer to be with your loved ones rather than mixing with lots of people.

Narrow margin at right of page

Extroverted and socially adaptable, you love the bright lights and people. Usually your energy level is good and you enjoy plenty of physical activities. You dislike being alone and having no one to talk to.

No margins

Could be you're too thrifty to let yourself go and enjoy having a good time. If your margins are almost non-existent you could be putting too much by for a rainy day — and this includes your emotional responses. Make sure that your economical streak doesn't become too obsessional.

Irregular margins

These indicate a love of travel and adventure, with reserve alternating with talkativeness. They also show ambivalent social attitudes. You are extroverted one moment and introverted the next, which could be confusing for those around you.

Narrow margin at top of page

There's a directness about your approach both to life and love that bypasses convention and you dislike being bothered by too many details. Playing according to the book isn't for you, but going straight for what you want is. There's also more than a hint of aggression in your make up.

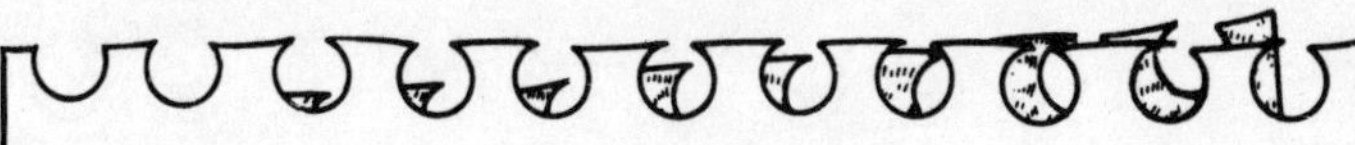

Wide margin to left of page

Generous, even extravagant, you love to make flamboyant gestures and give your friends surprise gifts. No one can boost your partner's ego better than you can and you are fully aware of your own worth and capabilities, both in your emotional and mental aspirations.

Narrow margin to left of page

Cautious and somewhat inhibited in your approach to life, you are afraid of making mistakes and show suspicion and a tendency to retreat into your corner at times. You need lots of reassurance from your loved ones in order to feel wanted and secure.

Wide margins all around

You are building walls against intrusion and this voluntary isolation could be losing you friends. If you have little desire to mix and socialise you could miss out on happiness and emotional satisfaction. However, you do possess a good sense of colour and love beautiful things.

ENVELOPE ADDRESSING

Where you place the address on the envelope will reveal a considerable amount about your personality. The envelope is divided into four parts and interpretation of the handwriting occurs from these four areas.

Position

Top left — Shows you are a day dreamer rather than a doer and often miss opportunities through this habit. Emotionally you are waiting for a knight in shining armour to sweep you off your feet.

Bottom left — Money minded and materialistic you often neglect your emotional needs in favour of your job or career.

Top right — Impulsive, warm and affectionate, you like to take the initiative and can be emotionally demonstrative and affectionate.

Bottom right — Indicates a love of adventure and a need to leave your past behind. Realistic and a trifle cynical, you are basically down to earth and have few illusions about life.

Size and shape

Small and cramped — This shows repression and a fear of getting involved. You could be bottling up your feelings instead of expressing them.

Address illegible — This shows a 'don't care' attitude. Lacking in harmony in your own life, you can't be responsible for anyone else's. Erratic and selfish, you are a rebel.

Capitals circled — This is a keep off sign, revealing that you want to be alone and need to feel secure before committing yourself to any course of action.

Underlining address — This stresses the importance you place on the contents inside the envelope, but you could be wasting too much time on trivial things and neglecting the realities.

Large writing — This reveals that you are an extrovert who wants to be the centre of attention. You have a strong need to express your personality in a flamboyant manner.

Small writing — This shows that your head is very much in control and you aren't keen on too much physical activity. In fact mental pursuits are more to your taste.

Unusually shaped letters — These show an original mind, but when they are badly formed or flourished with many whirls and circles they may show ostentatiousness and bad taste.

Left-slanted script — This is a sign of withdrawal, wanting to keep the world at bay.

Right-slanted script — This is a sign of sociability and friendliness.

An upright script — This shows independence and a good head for making decisions objectively.

If the writing on the envelope is the same as the writing on the letter inside, it shows you are just what you seem to be and don't put up any front in order to impress, but are reliable and honest.

PRESSURE IN HANDWRITING

Heavy pressure, going right through the paper so that an impression is left on the other side when you turn it over, shows plenty of vitality. The writer is energetic and influenced by the things he or she can see, feel and touch. Such writers are the doers of this world. They will like colour, movement, action and a sense of having a goal to aim for, as they are very goal minded. Persistent and persuasive, these writers live for today rather than the promise of things to come tomorrow.

Medium pressure is the most widely found. It shows a well balanced personality. The disposition is friendly, and the writer likes people and things, but rarely goes to extremes, either emotionally or socially, and doesn't make a show of enthusiasm or go into raptures easily.

These writers are able to adjust well to the world about them and are usually better adjusted than the heavy-pressure writer. They aren't too aggressive or ambitious in achieving their aims and can take things in their stride without getting into a flap. Less impatient and volatile, they can deal with problems with a good balance between mind and emotion.

Light pressure — this reveals highly sensitive people who are easily hurt and quick to take offence. Such writers have a strong critical sense, can be sarcastic under tension and enjoy being well thought of. Praise and encouragement tones down their sharpness. They can be reserved and rather prickly, choosing close friends with care.

Light-pressure writers tend to go for pastel shades and the lighter side of life than the heavier pressured writer. Emotionally they need affection more than sex. When the pressure is very light it can reveal frequent periods of fatigue and a lack of reserve energy to fall back on. Loyal and slightly conventional, they tend to distrust new ideas until proven.

Pressure which wavers — sometimes light, sometimes heavy — reveals an erratic personality with changing moods. Such people are unpredictable and often feel that they are under stress. Their feelings fluctuate like the wind and they are difficult to pin down to a course of action. Their highly emotional nature means that they can be difficult to deal with and to understand. These people find it hard to establish a routine and often their lifestyle is inclined to be disordered and lacking in harmony or stability.

INTROVERSION AND EXTROVERSION

Are you an introverted personality or an extrovert? Do you cling to the past and its influences or are you forward looking and adventurous? All is revealed by the slant of your handwriting.

The usual slant to the right shows an outgoing nature, sociability and an active goal-minded enthusiasm for the future.

If your handwriting slants more than 45 degrees it shows strong emotional impulses and needs. This is also linked to an over-excitable temperament and poor head control, particularly under stress or when your emotions are involved.

A left slant indicates introversion and self-consciousness. You live an active inner life and may have been influenced just that little too much in your early and formative years so that you find it hard to break away from this influence.

There is a certain amount of detachment in your nature as you often feel isolated and in the minority. Cautionary factors often prevent you from acting spontaneously and making intimate friends as you put up barriers as a defensive measure in order to protect your rather fragile ego. Sensitive and with strong family ties, you are often creative and artistic.

An upright script reveals that you are independent and self-reliant (in children's handwriting this shows good head control even at an early age). Your head rules your heart and you aren't easily swayed by your emotions or external influences.

Poise and a curious lack of empathy may make you appear far more controlled and cold than you are.

A mixed script, one that goes left, right and upright, reveals an erratic disposition and an inconsistent personality structure. You are frequently pulled in several directions at once and find it hard to stick to routine.

Strong emotional forces are often at the back of your unpredictable actions, with your emotional and mental natures fighting each other for dominance. Such mood variation is caused by your impressionability, especially to atmosphere, environment and people.

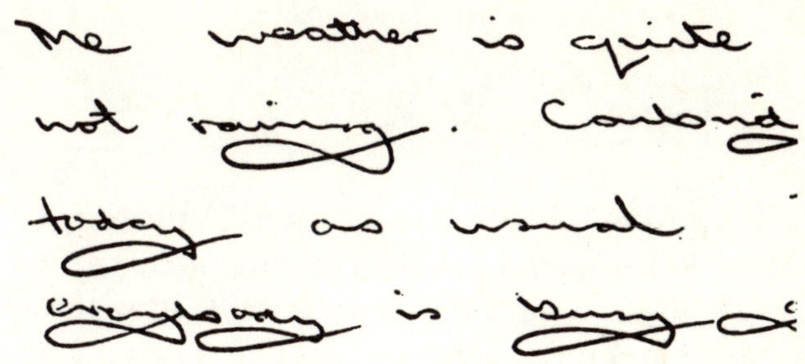

This extreme left slant shows introversion and a strong pull from past experiences. The swinging underlengths indicate a mother influence and the wide spacing between words is a sign of some emotional isolation.

The quick brown
jumped over the

This right slant is an indication of the writer's extroverted nature and desire to mix and meet socially. The rounded strokes reveal a warm, affectionate nature. The speed of the script indicates a quick thinking mind.

This upright script with its slightly angular strokes reveals good head control and a certain amount of aggression. The writer is straightforward and intelligent but inclined to keep emotions in check.

This erratic script going to the left then right shows inconsistency and belongs to an extremely moody personality who has difficulty in sticking to one task. The varying slant and size is often found in the handwriting of people who enjoy plenty of physical and mental activity.

This writer's rounded capital **I** shows a well developed sense of humour but the sharpening **t** bar crossing gives away a hasty temper.

RELEASED AND RESTRAINED WRITING FACTOR

The released or restrained factor in handwriting establishes the writer's personality. When the pen is held rigidly in the hand, the writing muscles are tense and this restricts the movement of the pen, causing the writing to be formed in a restrained manner, often appearing as a monotonous row of conforming letters, taut and controlled.

When the writing is flowing freely and smoothly, it shows fluency and vitality because of freedom of movement.

Most people's handwriting falls between the two; it is neither too rigid nor too loose, having characteristics of both, but not carried to extremes.

If your handwriting is controlled and rigid, your emotional life could suffer as you find it hard to relax and are often up-tight or anxious. Maybe you are conforming too much and doing what other people are expecting you to do rather than doing your own thing.

You find it difficult to express emotion spontaneously and usually your head rules your heart, making any impulsive gestures of affection appear to be 'soft'. Even though you may wish to let your loved ones know how much you care, you stifle your feelings. A more tolerant and relaxed attitude would release some of the pent up tension that your intenseness causes.

This rigid, controlled script shows the writer to be highly independent but repressed emotionally and unable to let her feelings out. She seeks to keep her feelings and thoughts under a firm discipline, and consequently misses out on life.

This left-slanted but narrow script is that of a far more relaxed writer, but still her tightly held feelings prevent her from showing a lot of warmth or affection. However, there are some rounded strokes indicating warmth, and the writer reveals excellent judgement in those unlooped underlengths.

This right-facing slant flows easily and without any restrictions. It has a rhythmic quality about it and is basically a symbol of the writer's need to communicate and find companionship — a reaching out to the world and other people. Such writers have a far more tolerant and spontaneous nature than the rigid script writer and can act with impulsiveness and warmth without embarrassment. Their feelings are more relaxed and outgoing and there is a need for affection.

better to have loved
to have loved at all.

Another rounded and right-facing script that reveals a feeling nature, warm and affectionate with a sensitive and perceptive streak. The writer is emotionally capable of many friendships and expresses her emotions freely. She is far happier in love than the restrained writer.

and I am looking
to that very much!

Although this script is rounded and basically non-aggressive, the writer's hand doesn't flow easily, as she holds on to her emotions. Kind and sensitive, she has an impressionable nature, seen in the open '**to**' and the left-sloping underlengths of her small **g**'s and **y**'s. She is hiding her true thoughts and feelings through a streak of cautiousness.

The most beautiful place in the world is

When the writing is slanting forward to the right and upward sloping, it shows a good social attitude, a need for communication, intelligence and rapid thinking.

This right-slanted script with its slightly angular strokes denotes an energetic person who is impatient and impulsive. Sociable but often irritable, he drives himself too hard. His emotional life could suffer through a careless attitude and lack of thoughtfulness.

RHYTHM IN HANDWRITING

The rhythm of handwriting gives the overall impression of the writing, and shows the physical, mental and spiritual forces of the writer. It expresses the writer's vitality and character and shows individual impulses which must be taken into consideration with other traits when evaluating personality. Harmonious and even handwriting denotes that the biological impulses of the writer are intact and that there is little in the way of physical or mental disturbance upsetting his equilibrium.

Unrhythmical writing, on the other hand, shows the writer who suffers from inner conflicts which have remained unresolved through his formative years into adulthood.

To grasp whether a sample of handwriting is rhythmic or unrhythmic, one looks at the connecting strokes, speed, spacing and formation of letters and slant. When there are large gaps between letters and words or varying slants within the writing showing changes of direction, there is irregular movement showing a disturbance. Such writers are restless, often suffering from anxiety (real or imagined) in their make-up. Because of lack of will power they are torn between impulses and control of the mind and emotion, resulting in poor self-control and restraint. On the more positive side, they may live an active inner life. This is the type of handwriting often found in artistic or creative people.

When the writing is flowing evenly and the spacing, pressure and size are well balanced, and the letters a reasonable height with the up and down strokes of approximate size, this reveals will power and self-control. The psychological impulses that influence the writer will result in the intellect becoming stronger than the emotions, making regularity possible.

Where there is over-control and the writing is rigid and without spontaneity, this can lead to obsessional behaviour and an almost compulsive inhibition, preventing the writer from developing into a more relaxed personality.

Very often young people adopt an irregular script in order to express their personality and leave the restraint of conforming behind them.

Rhythmic traits explained

These indicate the functional energies, their intensity, economy and scope in relationship to the will and impulses, which are important features in judging the mode of work and the scale of achievements.

Rhythmic writing stands for harmony and an even distribution of the emotions and impulses, and an economical use of energies, particularly when the rhythmic writing tendency is maintained throughout. But it must be remembered that a tendency to regulate can lead to compulsive behaviour and monotony, suppressing the personality.

Arrhythmic traits explained

These often indicate creative ability. There is often varying self-reliance and moodiness, an active mind, emotional intensity, impulsiveness under pressure, unreliability, instability of the sympathetic nervous system and abrupt changes of temper.

Showing an above average degree between pained experience, new constructive action, she also possesses deductive skill which enables several jumps ahead of her

Rhythmic handwriting. This right-slanted script with its well balanced zones shows a consistent mind and good head control.

it to Hamai's and saw the results on Thursday. I
this result, but of course I was hoping you would get an
rest of the results were not as good as we had hoped
difficult letter to write. remain [illegible]

There is an erratic slant to this script, indicating the writer's inability to remain consistent in thought and action. The varying slant, size and pressure all reveal a restless, mercurial mind.

sprwng apon me. I dont
work. Morning is my time.
If you have the incliation
be good to have a note
Now I must go to the

This very inflexible script reveals discipline and inhibition. The writer is unwilling to allow the emotions to get out of hand and maintains head control at all times to the detriment of spontaneity.

SPACING

The spacing between lines and words reveals whether the state of mind of the writer is erratic or orderly, i.e. whether he has clear or muddled thinking.

A well spaced letter with lines and words at an equal distance shows clear, mature thinking and the ability to assimilate emotional experiences and maintain integrity. It also shows good organising ability and a well developed planning capacity.

Emotional instability

If you space your lines and words poorly, this indicates emotional instability, your impulses dominating your intellect. You have a 'grasshopper' mind, jumping from one thing to another without order or method.

Very large spaces between lines and words are a sign of isolation. You may be feeling cut off emotionally and unable to communicate with others. This can also be seen in snobbish handwriting, where the writer is aloof and egotistically detached and lacking in spontaneity.

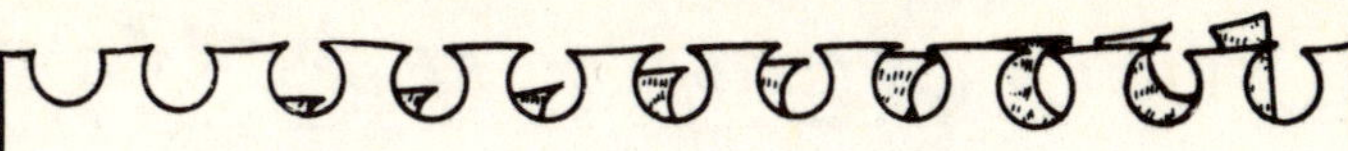

Very small spaces indicate the opposite, showing a need for contact and the companionship of other people.

If your handwriting has narrow spacing you could be feeling insecure and wish to become more involved at an emotional level. When the distance between lines and words overlaps, it reveals clarity for short distances only, and poor vision for planning ahead.

You are unable to stabilise your emotional responses and are often pulled in many directions at once, particularly if your slant fluctuates from left to right. You may be spontaneous in your reactions, but don't always see things clearly.

Really well balanced spacing should be of equal length between lines and words, showing self-assurance and a liberal mind with the faculty of discrimination and social confidence.

weather this week w.
that I work in this pa

This clear spacing shows excellent organising ability and judgement. The writer is able to discriminate in his intellectual and emotional life, and his social attitude is easy, comfortable and confident.

These spaces are almost non-existent. The text runs into confusion; each word and line is a jumbled mess. This shows that the writer is unable to think clearly and has difficulty in holding back emotional energy that demands release. There is little discipline indicated and yet the speed of the writing is quite fast, showing an intelligent mind but one that lacks the ability to check spontaneous impulses.

/and yet they drink they
But you say
in together raised

The large spacing between these lines and words shows an intelligent and somewhat aloof individual who enjoys a certain amount of personal privacy and who doesn't wish to mix socially unless there is a strong need to. Such writers are often artistic or creative and seek a degree of solitude to work in, regulating their sociability to their requirements.

I wonder what they
can make of my han

This average sized spacing which widens as the writer continues his letter shows an inconsistent personality — socially minded one day, reserved the next.

This rigid, obsessive script, with its non-existent or narrow spacing, indicates an introverted personality. There is a lack of conformity of the spacing, showing that the writer is inhibited and unable to live an active, socially integrated life.

Thread-like strokes joining words reveal a mentally agile thinker, but one who may skip over detail owing to haste and impatience. The writer is clever at solving problems but is inclined to manipulate and shows a tendency to be impetuous.

SIZE OF WRITING

Size of handwriting is of significance because it reveals whether you are a thinking person or a feeling person. The larger your handwriting, the more likely there is to be a sentimental and affectionate side to your nature, and an impulsiveness in the emotional area which could have a few repercussions.

Small writing is a sign of intelligence and analytical thinking and a tendency to allow the head to rule the heart. It shows that caution and responsibility are acting as a brake to impulsiveness and spontaneity.

Big writing is a sign of someone who needs a large, broad canvas to live and work in. It also indicates a strong need for self-expression and showing off, and a desire for attention and admiration. Such writers are unhappy in a restricted or repressive environment or relationship. They need to demonstrate their love and affection.

Exaggerated and large writing can reveal an obsessional nature, obstinate and difficult to deal with — someone who wants their own way and rarely considers other people.

Very small, almost minute writing reveals feelings of inferiority, the writer seeking to hide away from the limelight with no wish to be noticed. Such writers are often suffering from emotional upsets or experiences and influences in their early life which they find hard to shake off.

The most usual handwriting falls between the two and is a medium sized script showing a good balance between head and heart, impulse and control, able to maintain equilibrium between the senses and the mind.

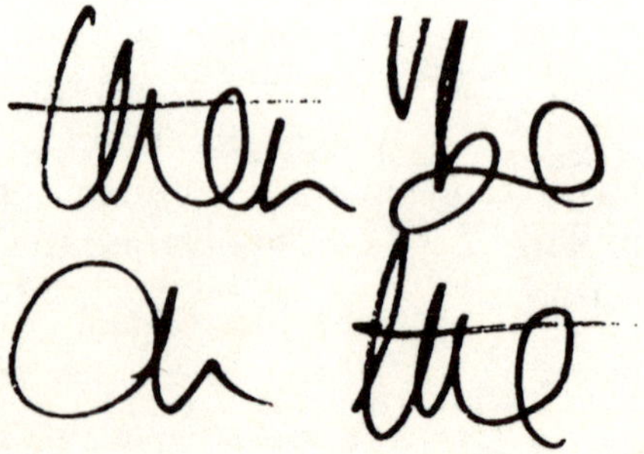

This huge script with its outsize letters shows an animated, over-zealous personality, fond of his own way and with an exaggerated ego.

The writer finds it hard to concentrate for long periods, is restless and likes to be seen and heard. Extravagant and over-active, there are signs in the heavy pressure of the writing of tension which the writer aggravates by a dominant and excessively impatient nature.

This script with its almost illegible letters indicates feelings of inferiority and a lack of confidence. The writer is afraid of making decisions and reveals a lot of inhibition both mentally and emotionally. He is incapable of socialising with ease because of his introspective nature and resulting lack of warmth of feeling. He has intellectualised everything, including his emotional needs.

This handwriting reveals an extremely social-minded personality. She is inclined to be over-generous, likes to entertain on a lavish scale and is very much aware of her own emotions. She is impatient, bored by details and enjoys plenty of attention. Basically non-aggressive but egotistical, she is materialistic and somewhat selfish in her attitude.

This medium-sized script shows a good balance between head and heart. The writer is able to distinguish between what is essential and what isn't in the social area and enjoys harmony whenever possible. There is no great urgency for self-expression and little domineering in the character structure.

This is the average size of handwriting used by most of the population.

STARTING AND ENDING STROKES

Those little strokes at the beginning of your words can reveal quite a lot about your personality, showing what sort of character you have and if you are a quick self-starter or a cautious individual.

A very long starting stroke indicates that you like to take your time preparing the way before tackling a new project and there's more than a hint of caution in your make-up.

If you start your words without any starting stroke you can get down to essentials rapidly and without fuss. Usually you are quick thinking and goal orientated, with an eye for detail and vision for planning ahead.

A hook at the beginning of your words indicates tenacity of purpose and a rather obstinate nature with firmly held opinions. You aren't easily swayed by other people and like to think you can't be influenced by them.

with my

A loop at the beginning of your words is a sign of jealousy. A small loop shows personal jealousy, a large loop, professional jealousy. Beware the writer who has a long angular stroke (starting in the lower zone) as he is going to be aggressive, assertive and egotistical, with a well developed critical sense and a poor sense of humour because he lacks tolerance.

Maybe

A starting stroke in the form of an arc means that the writer enjoys talking and likes the sound of his own voice. He needs to express his personality but can be dogmatic and inclined to have some very fixed ideas and opinions.

Ending strokes reveal whether you are socially minded or uncooperative, and whether you like to conserve your personal resources or have a tendency to meanness.

A long ending stroke indicates social awareness and generosity, but when the stroke is extended too much it can also show intolerance and a highly critical personality.

this is the

A hook at the end of your words shows egoism and an aggressive, even abrasive, nature together with a certain amount of defensiveness and a fighting spirit that doesn't like to admit any form of defeat.

No ending strokes but an abrupt halt to your words is a sign of brusqueness and severance of relationships or friendships without regret.

If your ending stroke reaches upwards (into the upper zone), you could be showing spiritual or religious leanings, even an interest in the occult.

When your ending stroke goes up and over to the left there's more than a hint of patronage in your attitude to others and you are inclined to be introspective.

An enrolled claw at the end of your stroke is a sign of greed and selfishness — often caused by early life experiences.

A stroke that goes to the left shows a hot temper and an unwillingness to compromise.

CAPITAL CLUES

Medium sized capitals show an objective valuation of self, therefore the capitals are important in handwriting analysis as a guide to the writer's feelings about himself and how he wishes to express his personality.

When the capitals are very large, and the writing of medium size, they show vanity, a high regard for self, pretentiousness and exaggeration. The writer dislikes the idea of being overlooked and desires to aim for individuality of style in his activities.

Many flourishes on capitals show a large ego and a vulgar form of conceit. Any exaggerated loop on a capital letter is a sign of self-love and superfluous mannerisms on the part of the writer.

Small capitals indicate concentration, a critical sense, intelligence and the power to assimilate facts, but they also reveal pettiness, over-scrupulousness, and often feelings of inferiority.

Narrow capitals indicate shyness and reserve, and often inhibition.

Broad and large capitals reveal wastefulness and vulgarity.

Original capitals express a high degree of intelligence and originality.

Simplification of capitals shows personal sincerity and intelligence, naturalness and the elimination of inessentials. The writer may be creative and can easily differentiate between what is important and what is unimportant, but he may lack an appreciation of anything that is not serving a purpose.

Different forms of the same capital letter in one sample of script can indicate versatility.

The capital I

The way you write your capital **I** reveals your ego rating and shows how you feel about yourself. Whether your **I** is small or large, angular or rounded, you are giving away quite a lot about your personality.

To check up on your ego rating, write a sentence with the word **I** in the middle — for instance, 'What sort of person am I revealing?' — and see what secrets you are letting out of the bag.

Your capital **I** is the most important thing you can write in handwriting analysis apart from your signature. It reveals how you wish the world to see you and how you feel about your standing in it.

I bought a

If your **I** is twice as large as the rest of your handwriting, it shows that you have a fairly high opinion of yourself and a healthy ego. You could be a little bit too overpowering when in a position of authority.

I have.

On the other hand, a small **I** reveals that you may be suffering from mild feelings of inferiority and don't always assert your personality when you should. Possibly, you need to come out of your shell and let your emotions run riot now and then.

I have

A printed capital **I** indicates a well balanced personality and an interest in literary matters. This familiarity with the printed word could be channelled into a creative sphere; it can show a cultured attitude to life.

that I would send

ysis. I think probab

An **I** written in form of a number 7 or 9 shows that money is often on your mind; it is important to you, or you may have a head for figure work. The material things of life mean much more to you and represent security and comfort.

I like

An **I** that is looped at the top shows a good sense of humour and an uncomplicated personality. You are excellent at sorting out other people's problems and your down to earth common sense means that you can cope with almost anything unexpected.

If your **I** is fragmented top and bottom this means that you are erratic and find it hard to maintain consistency in your life. You often have guilt feelings about the past, which influence your thoughts and actions. In your formative years there could have been a lack of environmental security which you constantly seek now as a compensation.

An **I** that is clawlike, with a stroke going back to the left, shows a love of money and the material things of life. You also try to avoid responsibility in your sexual life owing to apprehension and difficulty in establishing long-term relationships, yet you can be very protective towards your family.

An extremely slanting left-stroke **I** shows a guilt complex and often difficulty about discussing your emotional problems.

I — I — who

A complicated **I** shows self-awareness to a large degree. Wrapped up in your own little world and often putting up barriers against intrusion, you fail to take in other people's needs. There's plenty of affection in your nature and if channelled into friendships and wider horizons you can be sociable and loving.

I trust

An **I** in the shape of an **O** shows that you are frequently on the defensive and aren't too self-confident. Although you enjoy admiration and like to be liked, your shyness and introspective nature holds you back from making friends easily.

I missed you

If your **I** is rolled in two loops, this is a sign of protection. You are a little afraid of the outside world and somewhat suspicious of other people's motives. You may have been hurt in your emotional relationships and need to let go of your past experiences and start again.

I owe

An angular **I** is a sign of aggression. If this is your **I**, you want to be the one who is in charge of the home, and having an argumentative fight with your partner now and then adds a bit of excitement. You are also a good organiser and love to plan right down to the last detail.

I and

A huge, inflated **I** shows that you have an exaggerated ego and love to spread yourself around by showing off and giving vent to your sense of drama. You love to be the centre of attention and know how to express your personality to get noticed.

A straight **I** is a sign of good judgement and a desire to stick to essentials. You don't like fuss and, although not a romantic, you tend to be fatalistic in your relationships. An intelligent, capable and objective personality, you are able to eliminate the unimportant from the important and assume responsibility for a wide range of activity when necessary.

NUMERALS

It is often interesting to compare normal numbers with those used for money on cheques or bills which are frequently larger, denoting a concern with material values.

Smoothly written:

Shows a sober and serious attitude towards material values.

Small, sharp and concise:

Indicates a routine involvement in, and concentration on, money matters, often signifying an accountant or executive.

Indistinct:

Indicates a negligently indifferent or neurotic attitude to material values — sometimes a blurring of monetary issues in favour of the writer. Appears occasionally in blackmail letters.

Touched up:

A neurotic reaction, revealing financial anxiety and many problems.

Decorative:

A daydreamer who shies away from reality and financial matters.

Clumsy:

No concept of numbers — poor at maths. Could possibly neglect practical aspects.

THE SMALL LETTER t

When considering a specimen of handwriting, the small letter **t** can be a very important letter of the alphabet. No two people make exactly the same strokes.

Obviously in graphological analysis one has to take every single letter into account before an accurate analysis can be carried out, but the letter **t** reveals quite a lot about a writer's personality and especially his willpower or lack of it.

There are certain types of small **t** which can be recognised instantly as well known stroke formations, but it is the unusual **t** bar crossing that often has the graphologist foxed.

A low down **t** bar can indicate mild depression. If the stroke is weak, the writer may lack a strong will power. He finds it hard to make decisions and has little sense of responsibility or liking for assuming a dominant role. Care has to be taken here, because a weak **t** bar can also reveal poor health.

interest.

A very high **t** bar crossing is a sign of rising ambition, optimism and a desire to reach out for a goal. When the **t** bar is extra high it could reveal too much daydreaming on the part of the writer who lives in a fantasy world.

to

When the **t** bar is hooked, it shows great tenacity of purpose.

situation

A looped **t** bar crossing reveals sensitivity and a well developed critical sense. The writer is easily hurt, over-reacts under pressure and is liable to become anxious when tension builds up.

A **t** bar sloping to the left of the stem is a sign of caution and deliberation. Such writers rarely make impulsive gestures or act spontaneously; everything is carefully thought out. They are apprehensive about making mistakes.

handwriting

A **t** bar sloping down indicates sudden and unexpected anger. These writers possess a hasty temper and are extremely obstinate in the face of opposition. They also brood and are inclined to be rather moody and unpredictable.

obtained, intend to

A straight **t** bar of equal length each side of the stem reveals a good balance between mind and emotion. The writer is self-confident and steady with conscientious attention to detail, but no great dynamic thrust.

two of us.

A **t** bar flying to the right of the stem is a sign of a quick, agile mind, zeal and animation. There is a need for freedom of action and a dislike of restrictions.

Past with
e at his apt.

Watch out for the **t** bar crossing that has a triangular formation as it shows aggression and a lack of tolerance on the part of the writer. There will be a swift reaction to any form of rejection or emotional disappointment. This **t** bar is frequently found in the handwriting of people disappointed with their partner.

to

A heavy, thick **t** bar indicates energy and drive, but when the stroke is excessively heavy it can show a domineering personality, one who won't hesitate to use force as an argument.

A sharp-pointed **t** bar is a sign of a sarcastic and quick tempered personality. It also denotes an argumentative type, quick to take offence and blame others. This is often due to an in-built antagonism through hopes and dreams not being realised.

THE SIGNIFICANCE OF THE *i* DOT

Although it may appear small and insignificant in handwriting analysis, the **i** dot is of great value when looking for characteristics and individual traits. Because **i** dots are written unconsciously, they are often overlooked by the novice graphologist.

They are particularly interesting when they appear heavy in light pressure script, or light in heavy pressure script. In anonymous letters and forgery the writer can be detected when he or she doesn't disguise them.

A dot placed to the left of the stem shows strong links with the past and a tendency to procrastinate and to delay when decisions need to be made. There is hesitation indicated which could lose the writer opportunities.

An **i** dot made to the right of the letter reveals impatience and a mind set on a goal. The future rather than the past motivates and activates the writer's thoughts, feelings and deeds.

High flying dots indicate daydreaming and sometimes a lack of reality. They can show a certain hastiness in the writer's thinking process. They also demonstrate enthusiasm and zeal for new ideas although the writer may not have the consistency to carry them out.

Heavy **i** dots are a sign of mild depression and weariness. If they are extra heavy they can show anger caused by frustration — usually sexually or emotionally orientated.

Light **i** dots are a sign of a sensitive nature and, if very weak, a lack of physical strength and energy. They also reveal a good critical sense.

If your **i** dot is formed like a comma, this is a sign of a quick, agile mind. Usually it is found in a person of activity rather than deliberation. It can also show a love of attention and admiration as the writer likes to be well thought of and his self esteem is high on his list of priorities.

Should the dot be made in the shape of a small arc, this denotes a well developed intuition and excellent powers of observation.

An **i** dot made in the form of a dash shows aggression and irritability combined with speed of thought. Clever but impatient, the writer lacks tolerance and certainly won't suffer fools gladly.

A small circle above the stem of a letter is a sign of drama. The writer loves the limelight and desires to be noticed. He has a sense of fun and humour and enjoys showing off in a bid for attention. Usually this is a basically non-aggressive nature.

Varying **i** dots, fluctuating in slants and size, show mood variation and impressionability owing to emotional and environmental influences. The writer is often being pulled in several directions at once.

An **i** dot connected to the next letter shows a clever, intelligent and speedy mind with quick reflexes. The mental processes of such a writer are fluid and flexible.

Arrow-shaped dots indicate aggression and hostility with a touch of sarcasm, often acting as a defensive measure.

Weak **i** dots in strong writing reveal a character that is not consistently strong, while heavy pressure in light handwriting reveals adaptability and a sudden and unexpected temper.

No **i** dot made at all indicates a poor organising ability and a lack of order and method. Always in a hurry, the writer is apt to miss details and isn't always thorough in undertaking a task.

An **i** dot low down on the stem of a letter shows drooping spirits and a heavy heart.

Excessive dots can reveal an affected personality, vain and snobbish but trying to appear intellectual.

WHAT YOUR SIGNATURE REVEALS

Your signature is a symbol of how you wish the world to see you. Apart from the capital I, it is the most significant thing you can write. It reveals quite a lot about your character and what makes you tick.

A signature that has a vertical line at the end is a sign of caution and shows defensiveness and a desire to put up barriers against the world and people.

Tom Atkins

Beware the writer who circles a signature — this is a 'keep off' sign. These writers like to keep themselves to themselves and don't like mixing in or joining group activities.

John Blunt

An unadorned signature — no lines, curls or flourishes — shows you have an uncluttered mind. You are a clear, well cut and balanced individual, well able to stand on your own two feet. You are independent and mature.

Anna Morris

A signature sloping to the right shows an outgoing personality, friendly and forward looking with a need to join in and communicate.

Clare Harrison.

A signature sloping to the left indicates shyness or reserve, and a holding back because of a pull from past experiences and influences.

Henry Black.

A very large signature is a sign of a flamboyant nature, an exaggerated ego structure and often a bossy, thoughtless personality.

Mary Soames

A small signature reveals modesty and good mental powers. When it is too small and cramped it can indicate inferiority feelings.

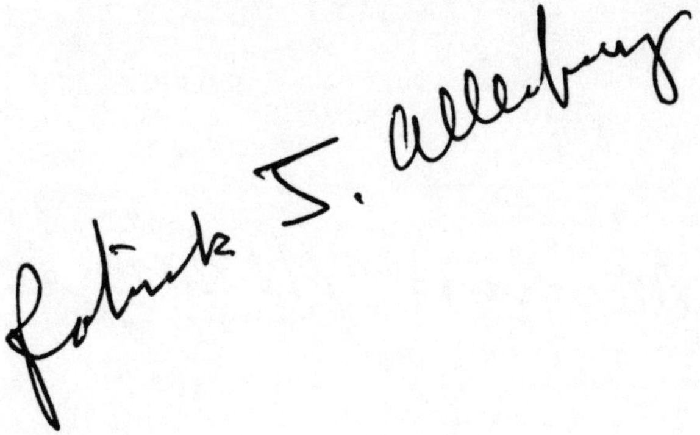

A rising signature shows optimism on the part of the writer while a descending signature shows pessimism.

If the signature is the same size as the rest of the script it means the writer is just what he or she seems to be and doesn't put on false airs and graces.

A very heavy pressure in a signature is a sign of energy and vitality, while a light pressure signature reveals a highly sensitive and easily hurt nature.

Angular strokes in a signature are a sign of aggression.

Rounded strokes belong to the more affectionate and warm hearted personality.

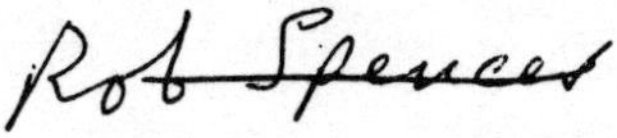

Crossing out or crossing through a signature is a sign of unhappiness and rebellion, and often anger directed either against the world or the writer.

A legible signature is always a sign of sincerity and reliability, while an illegible signature can denote a certain amount of deception.

Adding a full stop of comma indicates a conventional and rather pedantic person. It also shows caution. Because the signature is written by many people much more than any other word, it is often written very quickly, especially if it has to be written several times a day. This can be misleading when analysing characteristics from handwriting as an uneducated hand may well have a well written signature.

A signature that is entirely different from the rest of the script shows a discrepancy between the outer personality and the inner, the conscious and the unconscious.

Placing a signature to the right of the page reveals activity and action, and a desire to go forward. Placing it to the left is a sign of a need for security and often disappointment so that the writer retreats into self, an escapist attitude.

A signature placed in the middle of the page reveals a personality with a good balance between mind and emotion and one who really lets his or her emotions get out of hand without due thought for the consequences.

Underlining a signature is a sign of the writer's desire to stress his importance and is an ego emphasis.

SOME EXAMPLES OF HANDWRITING ANALYSIS

Sample 1

my handwriting is
very good. I was tau
to write this way at s
and my handwriting
changed much.
But I would
to know what you mc

This rather cumbersome script with its copy-book formation reveals a slightly immature personality. The roundness of the letters indicates a passive rather than active individual and the left slant shows some shyness. The pressure is inclined to vary from medium to light, a sign of an inconsistent thinker, and the loops at the top of the small **h**'s show day-dreaming.

The writer lacks spontaneity and finds it hard to be decisive, resulting in procrastination. The looped **t** bar crossing indicates sensitivity, while the arcade-shaped small **m**'s and **n**'s show a slightly secretive nature. There is a little nervousness revealed in the overstroking and the lines are far too close together, always signifying poor organising ability and a tendency to lack objectivity.

This is not a good form level handwriting and the rhythm is erratic.

Sample 2

This bold, energetic and confident writing shows executive qualities of organisation and initiative. The writing is well spaced, has excellent pressure and shows a highly intelligent and socially minded personality who is able to keep his personal reserve and yet communicate with skill.

and I could thus join you on
Monday March 1st.

I look forward very much to
receiving your confirmation and
the photographs you promised me

With best regards,

The closed small **o**'s are a sign of an ability to keep his own counsel and the well formed capital **I** shows a strong ego structure.

This writer is outgoing and optimistic and is highly motivated. He likes a challenge and knows how to maintain discipline and accept responsibility.

There is individuality in some of his letters and a firm, yet adaptable approach to life and its problems. The pointed downstrokes indicate his need for material security, the rounded middle zone letters his need for emotional and environmental security.

Sample 3

Meryl is intelligent and very well organised; her handwriting is fast and well spaced. The good rhythm shows her ability to maintain discipline and a consistent pattern of behaviour. There is sensitivity in the light pressure and the nicely balanced zones are a sign of judgement. The right slant shows her to be a friendly, outgoing and socially active personality who enjoys meeting and mixing with people.

departure for 24 hours which meant
extra expense – luckily we got our room
for another night as incoming guests were
obviously delayed too
will try to meet you some time – it
would be nice to see you –
All good wishes — also from Karl.
Meryl

The long looped lower zone letters are a sign of a need for both emotional and material security and the little starting strokes reveal an innate caution.

The writing is slightly thread-like in the middle of her words, always a sign of talent for dealing with people, tact and diplomacy.

The arc over her small **i** demonstrates her excellent powers of observation.

Her signature is the same as the rest of the script, showing that Meryl is just what she seems to be and doesn't put up any facade or hide behind a mask; her private and public life are the same.

Sample 4

This highly intelligent writing with its speed and thread linkage shows a hasty, impatient, yet clever personality who has extremely good manipulating ability. He uses his psychological talent to aid him in assessing people.

The analyst helped me to
decide the right course to take.
As a psychedelic morer I think
my original idea worth pursuing.
Your analysis confirms my reasoning
I have not yet decided which

The right slant shows a socially adaptable disposition prevails, and the linking together of words is always a sign of mental skill.

The straight capital **I** reveals an ability to get down to essentials quickly and without fuss. The large spaces indicate organising and planning capabilities; the small arc over the **i** shows observation.

This is the handwriting of a man who has considerable enthusiasm and who will tackle fresh ideas and concepts with determination.

Assertive and yet with a degree of empathy showing in his script, this writer has an independent and forthright nature, is able to accept responsibility and has good judgement.

CHECK YOUR SOCIAL RATING

Doodling faces

If you want to check up on your social rating, have a look at the type of face you doodle when in an idle moment you have a pen in hand and a writing surface near by.

The face you doodle can give clues to how you react to other people, your friends and family, showing if you are outgoing and sociable or reserved and shy.

Faces that are turned to the left of the page show a degree of shyness or reserve: you may have difficulty in establishing relationships, or friendships, owing to past experiences which have influenced you. Possibly introspective as a child, you need to come out of your shell so that you can mix and communicate with confidence. Socially you often take a back seat, joining a group or class will work wonders.

If your faces look to the right of the page you are forward thinking and socially minded although often unaware of the people around you and their feelings. You get new ideas and are keen to start fresh projects, but you don't always think of the consequences owing to impulsiveness. This can lead to a few social upsets which you are quick to handle as you enjoy using your ability to extricate yourself from difficult situations.

A full face shows you to be socially adept and friendly, with lots of friends and acquaintances, as you can mix easily without effort. Check up on the sort of face you doodle however, from the samples shown, as they do vary. You enjoy being part of the crowd and are usually liked and made welcome within your group or family circle.

Unhappy faces, ugly faces and those with distorted features are often signs of anger, frustration or unhappiness with your present lifestyle. You could be having an emotionally disturbing relationship which is causing you anxiety and this could affect your social attitude and mood variation.

Kindly, smiling faces with plenty of detail are a sign of an affectionate and happy, contented personality, but if your faces wear glasses, or a moustache, you could be concealing a secret or two.

Beware the doodler who draws a pipe or cigar in the mouth of his face and uses heavy pressure, as this is often a sign of pent up anger or aggression. Sometimes it signifies tension. This is symbolic of someone who wants to keep his distance and is inclined to be dogmatic and rather opinionated.

Young girls often doodle idealised self-portraits, a symbolic desire for beauty revealing that they want to be thought of as glamorous and alluring. Occasionally these are doodled with long flowing hair and exaggerated eyelashes.

If your doodle has a mouthful of teeth you could be wrestling with a sexual problem that's bothering you, as teeth are frequently symbolic of frustration or sexual anxiety. This could affect your social life.

Tightly sealed lips to your doodled face indicates inhibition and emotional withdrawal, but nicely formed, generous lips are the opposite, revealing warmth and love.

This left-facing doodle with its sharp nose shows a strong pull from past experiences which the doodler finds hard to let go of. She is inclined to be reserved, and yet the open mouth indicates that she has a desire to mix and communicate.

This wish-fulfilment doodle shows with its long flowing hair and eyelashes that the doodler wants to project a romantic and glamorous image of herself, yet the left slant shows that she is somewhat shy, and not as sociable as she would like to be.

This full, spiky looking face shows an off-beat sense of humour and a tense, mildly aggressive personality with strong critical faculties. The tightly closed mouth indicates inhibitions in the emotional area, and this doodler bottles up his true feelings.

This right-facing doodle with beard and tumbled hair reveals a degree of friendliness and sociability combined with caution and no hang-ups about the past. He knows where he's going and makes straight for his goals.

There is a nicely balanced sense of harmony in this face, with its hat and feather. The smiling countenance shows a happy, friendly disposition, looking out at the world with kindliness.

Another full face with a smiling countenance and well rounded strokes, showing a sense of humour and fun. The doodler is open, generous and friendly.

The large teeth shown in this doodle indicate some sexual problems are bothering the doodler and he feels hostile to the world in general.

AN ASSORTMENT OF DOODLES

An excellent way of analysing yourself is by looking at doodles to see what form they take and where on the page you position them.

To the left of the page lies the past, and its emotional and environmental experiences; to the right lies the future. If your doodle is in the middle of the page, you enjoy being in the heart of things. But if your doodle is small and isolated and in the middle, beware, you could be keeping the world at bay.

Whenever you find yourself doodling refer to the following samples and you may discover something new about yourself. Remember, whether you are left or right-handed, the graphic significance of your doodle is the same.

Tiny houses

Houses with smoke coming out of the chimney shows a need for security, home and family. This doodler is saying very plainly that she wants a husband, home and children, and a quiet and peaceful existence with her loved ones around her. She is not ambitious for herself but has plenty of help and encouragement to offer those who are close to her.

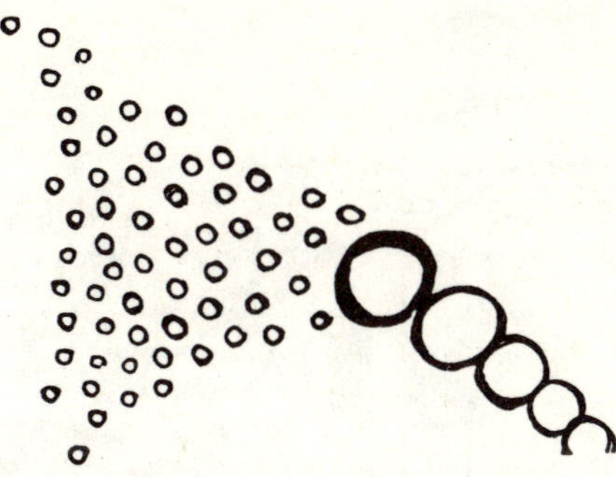

The ring

This is a sign of ever-lasting love and affection. This doodler has a great need to give and receive love. There are no angular strokes to the doodle, so she isn't aggressive. In fact, she loves harmony in her relationships.

Boxes

Making boxes or boxes within boxes, indicates a constructive mind. The doodler has the ability to carry out many ideas and suggestions but isn't likely to take on anything she can't handle. She is clear about her aims and ambitions but emotionally she feels trapped. She allows her head to rule her heart and she's not easily diverted from her chosen path.

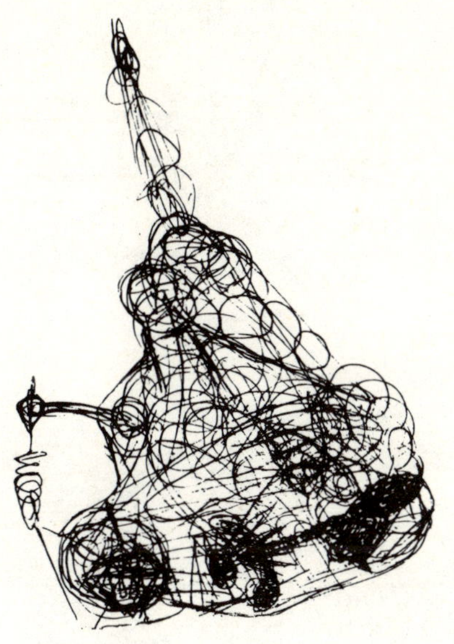

Filled-in doodle

A sign to beware of, as these doodles indicate a mild fear or apprehension that is worrying the doodler. Very often this is in the emotional area and reveals tenseness and anxiety about relationships. The filled-in squares show the writer is feeling somewhat trapped and is trying to solve his problems by devious means.

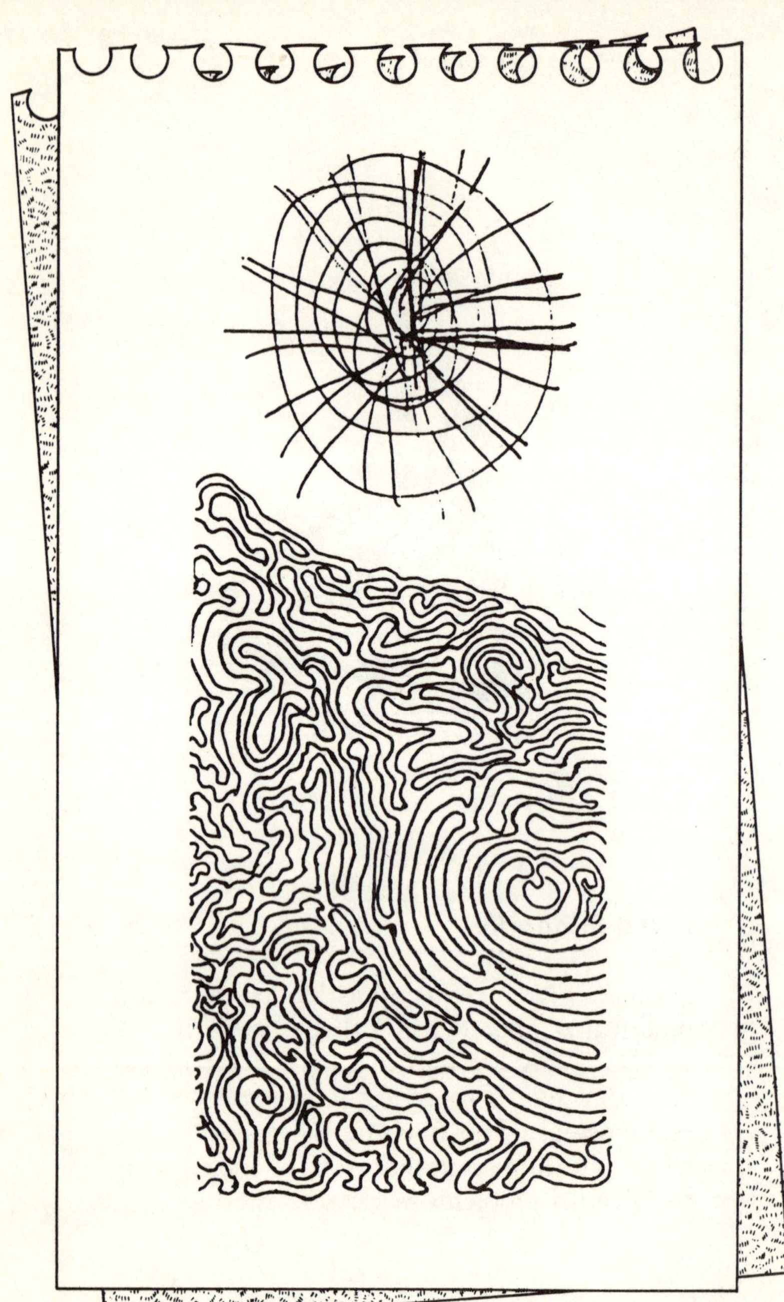

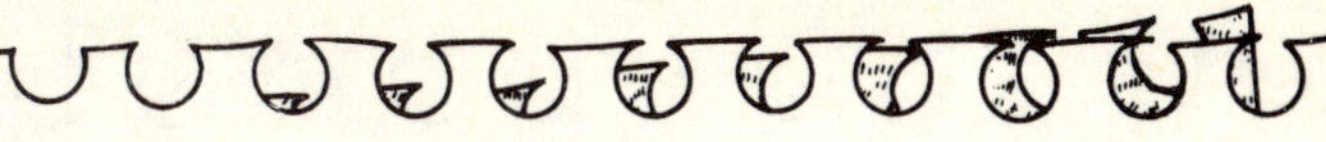

Mazes or webs

These very often reveal that the doodler seeks to find a solution to a problem. These are subconscious symbols of feeling caught and trapped. The heavier the pressure, the more worried the writer demonstrates himself or herself to be.

Animals

Furry animals show that you are sentimental and kind, with a very emotional nature. You long to belong and are inclined to be emotionally gullible at times. Basically a non-aggressive personality, you like harmony and stay away from friction as any form of conflict can cause you anxiety.

Money

Money symbols, the pound sign or dollar sign, doodled over and over again, mean that you may be obsessed with money and what it can or can't do. This symbol is also seen occasionally in the doodles of people who are working in financial areas.

Fish

Fish, snakes and crocodiles are sensual symbols in doodle analysis, when drawn by women, and show a subconscious preoccupation with sex and sexual thoughts and longings.

Vehicles

Cars, aeroplanes and ships show a desire for travel and to seek new adventures, new places and new ideas. It is an unspoken wish to get away from routine and the humdrum of life for a while and explore new horizons.

Wavy lines

Wavy lines indicate a love of movement and travel, expressive gestures and dancing. Many actresses and dancers, even singers, often scribble this design.

Watching eyes

Watching eyes in doodle analysis are symbolic of a suspicious nature. They reveal a certain amount of mistrust and resentment and often this is directed towards the doodler's partner. Filled-in irises show a clever but suspicious nature and some hostility towards the world.

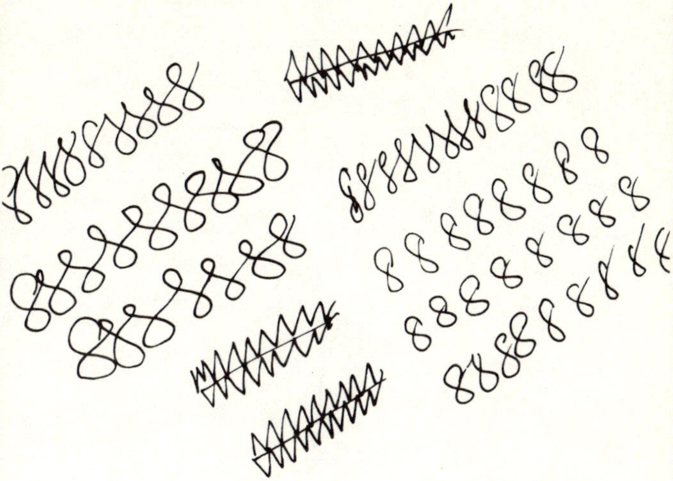

A repetitive design

This doodle shows a careful and logical mind. The doodler is practical and down to earth with an excellent eye for detail. She is consistent and not likely to act in a hasty manner. As her complicated design has angular strokes, she can be slightly aggressive at times. Cautious about committing herself, she is timid in the emotional sphere but she can be loyal and loving with the right partner.

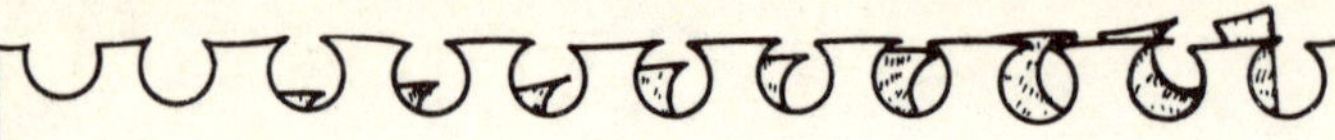

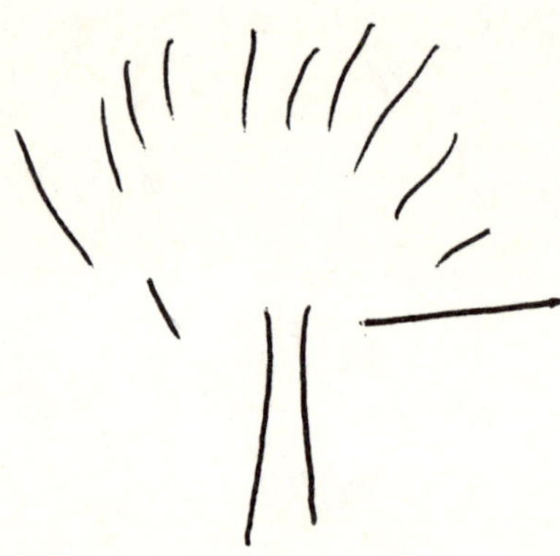

Spiky tree

This spiky tree shows a doodler who is strong willed and stubborn. She's also under a degree of strain or tension. She may not realise this consciously but it's there. It shows in the sharp, angular strokes. She has a slightly bitter attitude to life and love. People who doodle this type of tree are usually a bit sarcastic and have a sardonic sense of humour. They are also very orderly and extremely definite in their likes and dislikes, which they form on first impressions. The general feeling is of a disposition that's rather 'touchy'.

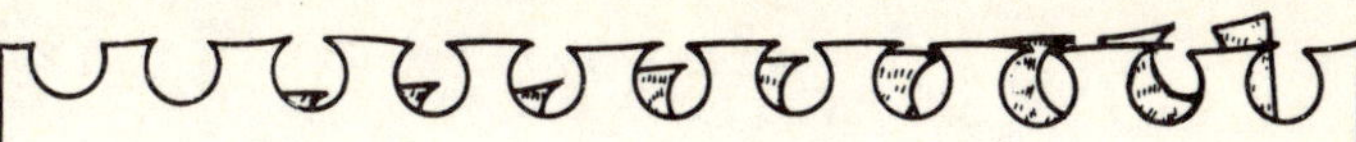

Fluffy tree

This large, rounded, fluffy tree is a sign of sociability and an active social life. The writer likes to be the life and soul of the party and is basically a non-aggressive, friendly and kindly personality. However, there is a tiny hint of superficiality in her feelings at times. She is a born romantic.

Cats, flowers, hearts

Cats, flowers and hearts here all indicate the person who is in love with love. Sentimental and possessing a great deal of affection, the doodler enjoys plenty of love and tends to daydream. Sometimes lacking a sense of reality, she is gullible and sometimes taken in, especially in romantic affairs.

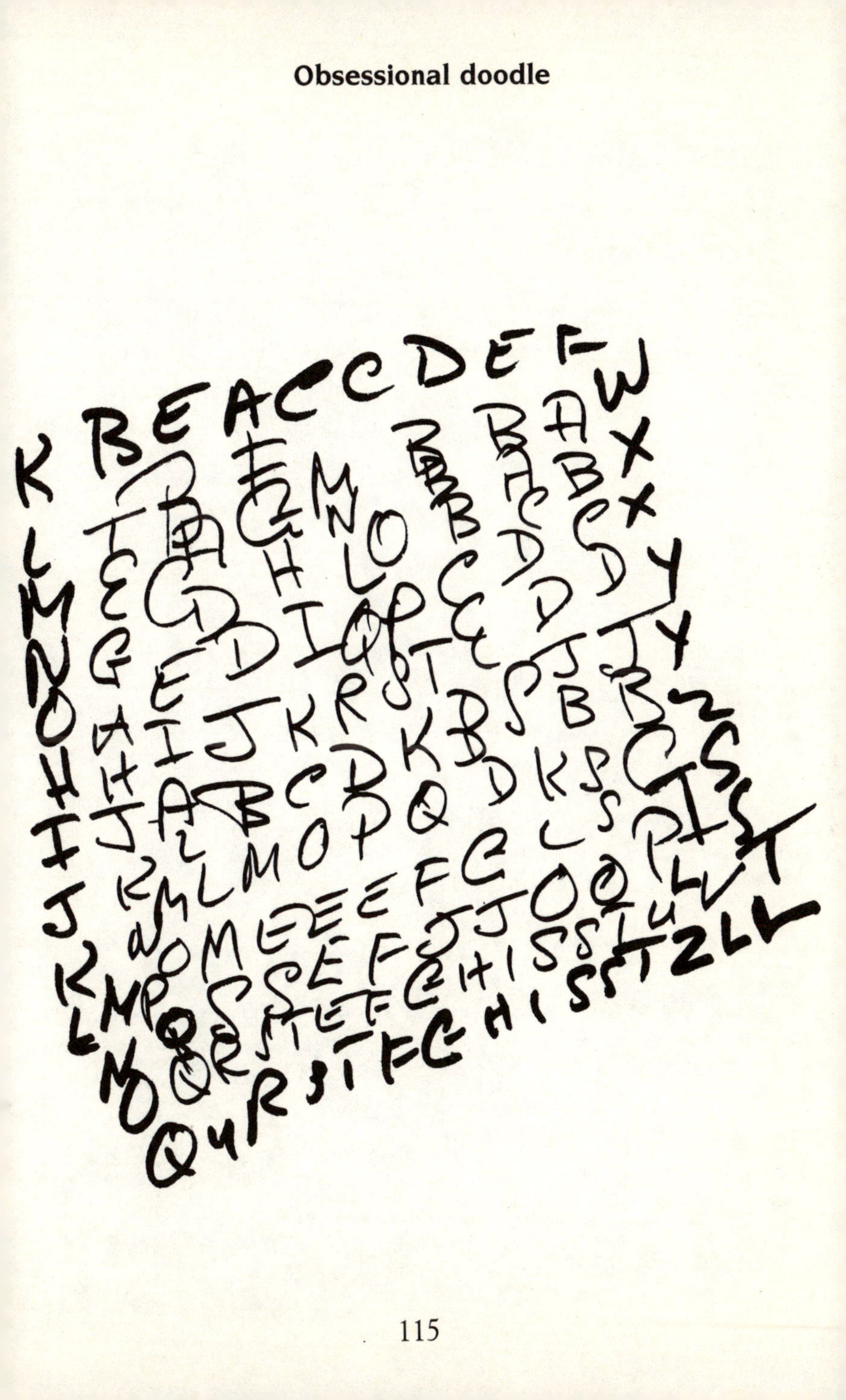

Obsessional doodle

Versatile doodle

A GUIDE TO GRAPHOLOGICAL TRAITS

What to look for

Ambition: Sloping lines going upwards, long downstrokes to letter **g** and **y**. Good pressure.

Analytical ability: Small writing, neat margins and angles. Medium pressure.

Arrogance: Large inflated capitals, especially in the signature. Flourishes and whirls, **t** bars inflated and capital **I** exaggerated.

Brutality: Large, sharpened **t** bars, leftward tending strokes. Heavy pressure.

Business acumen: Small, even letters, well formed loops, angular or arcade formation of letters. **M** and **n** sharpened at top. Slightly rising **t** bar to right.

Conscientiousness: Legible handwriting and well formed letters, without too many loops or exaggerations. Even middle zone and good rhythm. Carefully placed **i** dot.

Discipline: Well balanced writing, small letters (nearly all same size). Even flow of pressure.

Egoism: Huge capitals, underlining of signature and large middle zone letters.

Emotionality: Right-slanted writing, full of wide loops both on upper and lower strokes. Medium pressure.

Frankness: Small **a**'s and **o**'s open at top, right slant, quick writing.

Generosity: Large spacing between letters and width between lines well balanced.

Honesty: Right-slanted, legible handwriting. No left tendencies. Signature same as script, with no discrepancies.

Hypocrisy: Poorly formed letters with flat small **m** and **o** open at bottom.

Independence: Upright or slight right slant. Bold, firm capitals, straight capital **I**. Medium pressure.

Inferiority complex: Small script, left slant and some thread writing. Narrow margins, small capital **I**. Light pressure.

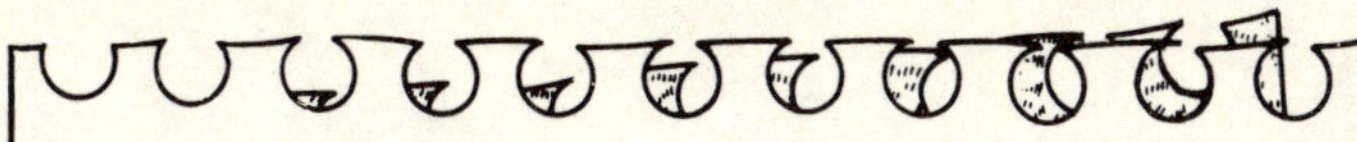

Intuition: Breaks between letters. Fast writing with different forms of connection, **i** dots joining other letters together.

Jealousy: Small circle at the beginning of capital **M** or **N**.

Logic: All letters well connected. Even baseline and small script.

Materialism: Large underlengths and loops with strong pressure. Money sign sometimes in capitals.

Maturity: Lack of embellishments, upright strokes, speedy script and small writing.

Meditativeness: Arcade script, upright strokes and slow rhythm.

Optimism: Upward sloping script with speed. Well proportioned letters with legible strokes.

Organising ability: Good spacing, clean margins and no tangling of lines.

Pessimism: Drooping writing, sloping downwards and low **t** bar crossing.

Pettiness: Angular strokes, thin writing. Triangular underlengths and **t** bar crossing.

Seclusion: Wide margins, with large spacing between words and lines.

Secretiveness: Closed and knotted small **a**'s and **o**'s. Arcade small **m**'s.

Sensuality: Pasty writing, thick strokes and varying pressure on underlengths of **g** and **y**.

Talkativeness: Open small **a**'s and **o**'s at the top. Right slant and narrow margins, especially to the right of the page.

Vanity: Large capitals, broad letters in middle zone, inflated capital **I**.

Weak-willed: Light pressure, poorly formed **t** bar and faint **i** dot.

Worrier: Spiky writing, thin pressure and angular lower loops.

Yielding: Garland writing with medium pressure and wide spacing between letters.

Zeal: Lively writing, right slant, good pressure and rising lines.

IDIOSYNCRATIC FEATURES

Idiosyncratic features are those traits special to a particular writer, made by subconscious movements of the hand, and which help establish the writing style.

These features, arising from the depths of the personality, are so automatic, that the writer isn't aware that he does them. So used are we to writing the way we do, adding little bits and pieces to our script, we would find it hard to disguise our writing completely if we tried.

Sometimes it may be necessary to use a magnifying glass to detect idiosyncratic features; they can be quite insignificant and are often overlooked. Not all samples of handwriting have them as not all people do them. But in forgery or questioned documents and anonymous letters they can be an added means of detection.

The most usual idiosyncratic features are: letters written the wrong way round, especially the small letters **b** and **d**; dots placed after words whether grammatically correct or not; a changing writing angle from left to right in the middle of a word (or right to left); capital letters in the middle of a word (the capital letter **R** occurs very commonly).

When looking for these features it is important to scrutinise as many samples of the writer's handwriting as possible, even going back a couple of years or so.

Letters written the wrong way round point to mental strain. Dots placed after a name are a sign of caution, and dots placed arbitrarily in either upper or lower zone reveal guilt feelings. A dot is always an inhibitive sign in handwriting.

The capital **R** written in the middle of a word instead of a small **r** shows a significant bid for attention, by people who feel neglected or overlooked, or who have a desire for self-expression.

A dot made in a circle above the **i** can also show a need for self-expression and is frequently added to the stem by young women who wish to draw attention to themselves.

A writing angle that changes left to right indicates parental conflict in the writer's formative years, leaving unresolved emotional problems.

Idiosyncratic features

M	**Written as**	m
Q	**Written as**	Q
S	**Written as**	2
b	**Written as**	d
d	**Written as**	b
i	**Written as**	i
I	**Written as**	İ
A	**Written as**	A

Graphology NOTES

Graphology NOTES

Concise Graphology Notebook – Index